LOOK AT YOURSELF AND
ACCEPT WHO YOU ARE

LOOK AT YOURSELF AND ACCEPT WHO YOU ARE

A step-by-step guide to learning to love yourself, embrace your reality and live the present to the fullest

The Wellness Factory

At The Wellness Factory *we believe that physical, emotional and intellectual well-being is a fundamental right that we cannot do without. All dimensions of our existence are important and deserve to be cared for with equal concern. We do our part to help you reconnect with yourself and live an ever more fulfilling life.*

We have written this book for you with care, love and with the desire that it will be helpful. If you find any typos, remember that we are as human as you are.

What you resist – persists. What you accept – transforms.

Carl G. Jung

Table of Contents

THE SAME DOOR OPENS TO ANOTHER WORLD

During our first steps in life we accept everything with wonderful curiosity: our body, our environment, our being. It does not mean that there are no pains, discomforts; but in general, we embrace the world with a connatural fullness.

The context, the passing of the years, judgments, life's disappointments, etc., gradually move us away from this natural state to the point that we begin to feel rejection towards our surroundings, towards life itself and even towards ourselves.

This is not a minor detail. There is no fullness of life without acceptance. Accepting what we are, what happens to us and also what does not happen to us is the way to enjoy life, not to resign ourselves but to understand it and to change what is possible to change. And if we cannot do it (because not everything can be changed despite what the self-help gurus say), to learn to look at life with different eyes. Or in other words, to enter a different world using the same door.

We like to refer to acceptance as self-acceptance, because in that way it implies that change is always within oneself.

Self-acceptance is an emotional and psychological process that involves accepting and valuing oneself as one is, with all one's strengths and weaknesses, virtues and defects. Self-acceptance involves recognizing and accepting our emotions, thoughts and behaviors, without judging or criticizing them in a negative way.

This does not mean that we should be satisfied with all aspects of our lives or ourselves. Instead, it is about recognizing that we are imperfect human beings, that we all make mistakes and that we can learn and grow through our experiences. Self-acceptance also involves having a positive and loving attitude towards oneself, rather than a critical and negative attitude. This can help us increase our self-esteem and develop greater self-confidence.

We must realize that we are human and that it is perfectly okay to make mistakes; on the contrary, we can use our mistakes as learning opportunities to better understand ourselves and strive to improve, appreciating our successes and celebrating our achievements, no matter how small they may be.

Accepting ourselves is to learn to look at ourselves in all the dimensions of our life.

Accepting ourselves is a process of self-knowledge that leads us to discover who we really are, taking into account our story, our achievements, failures, emotions, thoughts, relationships, differences, etc. It is also about accepting our body, our scars, our imperfections, our way of being, our individuality and our diversity. It means learning to look at ourselves with love, compassion and respect, living with our limitations and giving ourselves permission to grow, learn and evolve.

It is true that our limitations can deceive us, as they can make us believe that we cannot achieve something when in fact we can. This can lead to negative results, such as lack of motivation to do new things or insecurity when trying things that have not been done before. Therefore, it is important to be aware of our limitations and try to overcome them, so that we can achieve our goals and succeed.

Our thinking contains the germ of all our victories and defeats.

We all have many hidden skills, talents and knowledge within ourselves that we often don't know we have.

These can be as varied as creative writing, painting, computer programming, cooking, dancing, photography, leadership, communication skills, etc. These talents can be discovered through practice, learning and experimentation.

There are many of us who find it difficult to accept ourselves; self-acceptance can be a difficult process. However, it is important to remember that we are all unique and that is something to celebrate. Try to find things you like about yourself and focus on that,

This process can be challenging because it involves an emotional and psychological process that requires a great deal of self-reflection and self-compassion. Often, we find it easier to judge and criticize ourselves rather than accept ourselves unconditionally.

Self-acceptance also involves dealing with our own limitations, flaws and weaknesses, which can be uncomfortable and challenging. We may have to face our negative emotions, such as shame or fear, and learn to embrace and accept these feelings without judging or criticizing them. Another challenge is the pressure from society and culture to meet certain expectations and ideals. This can hinder the process of self-acceptance, as we often compare ourselves to others and judge ourselves for not meeting certain standards.

Accepting ourselves is a learning process that never ceases as human beings as we change our thoughts, habits and context.

Throughout these pages, this guide will accompany you in the process of learning to accept and love yourself; to understand that you have faults and qualities, and that both are important; to work to improve the areas in which you are not so comfortable with yourself, such as your self-esteem, your level of confidence and your relationship with others; to allow love and respect to flow from the inside out; to weigh positively, as positive thoughts become positive actions; to embrace your limits, without ever giving up dreaming and working; and to work to improve the areas in which you are not so comfortable with yourself. It will also help you to allow love and respect to flow from the inside out; to weigh positively, as positive thoughts turn into positive actions; to assume your limits, never stop dreaming and working; to learn from your experiences and from life; to love your body and discover all its possibilities; and, above all, to enjoy your life.

WHY IS SELF-ACCEPTANCE SO CRUCIAL?

Self-acceptance is essential to our emotional well-being and personal development. **By accepting ourselves, we free ourselves from the weight of external expectations** and can begin to value our own worth and uniqueness.

Self-acceptance helps us build a strong and coherent identity by recognizing our strengths, limitations and needs. It allows us to develop a kinder and more tolerant attitude towards ourselves, thus cultivating our self-esteem.

Likewise, self-acceptance allows us to have a **more realistic perspective of ourselves** and the world around us, which can reduce stress and anxiety in our lives. By learning to accept ourselves, we are better equipped to deal with difficult situations and make important decisions.

Self-acceptance is also important for our relationships with others, as it allows us to be more authentic and genuine in our interactions. By having a more positive and loving attitude toward ourselves, we are also more likely to have a more compassionate and tolerant attitude toward others.

The first step toward acceptance is **self-knowledge**. This means having a clear understanding of who you are, your strengths and weaknesses, as well as your values and beliefs. Self-knowledge helps you make informed decisions about how you want to live your life and identify any areas of your life that need improvement. This allows you to understand and accept your limitations, as well as those things you cannot change, without being too hard on yourself and taking a realistic approach to your life.

By knowing yourself, by realizing that you are a being with contradictory emotions, thoughts and desires, you can begin the journey. And along the way, of course, you will get to know yourself more and more.

Let's walk together, and above all walk with yourself, with confidence, with enthusiasm and with passion for the life you have been given.

STEP ONE:
ACCEPT WHO YOU ARE AND WHO YOU WANT TO BE

Before accepting the person who dwells inside you, it is important to accept the body that this person occupies, that is, you, that is, your own body.

Accepting your body has a significant impact on your emotional well-being and overall quality of life. By accepting it, you can learn to feel more comfortable in your own skin, improve your self-esteem and foster a more positive attitude towards your body and yourself.

Body acceptance can also help you cultivate a healthier relationship with food and exercise. **By accepting your body as it is, you can learn to**

listen to its needs and nourish it properly, rather than punishing yourself or subjecting yourself to extreme dieting and exercise that can be detrimental to your health.

In addition, body acceptance can help you free yourself from judgment and comparison to others. By accepting your body as it is, you can stop comparing yourself to the beauty ideals promoted by society and **focus on being the best version of yourself**.

This also fosters a more positive and caring attitude towards others; you can develop a greater understanding and empathy for the different body shapes and sizes of the people around you, and foster a culture of inclusion and respect.

Accepting our body as it is, is a difficult task but essential to have a better quality of life. First, we must learn to be kind to ourselves and accept ourselves as we are. This means **not comparing ourselves to others** and being proud of our unique characteristics and qualities. It is important to focus on what makes us unique and special, rather than on what is missing.

You are special not because you are different. In reality, there are many people like you. **What is special about you is that ability to see others as unique**.

Your true value is in your eyes. And if you project that same look onto yourself, you will value and love yourself a lot.

Using positive affirmations, practicing relaxing activities and finding healthy ways to express and endure our emotions will help us feel better and accept ourselves as we are.

It is important to remember that the body is a great source of pleasure and should not be seen as something negative. The freedom of expression of our body is a gift and a way to enjoy life.

Make a list of the things you like most about your body. Now think about skills linked to your body, such as strength, dexterity, agility, gracefulness.

A body does not only consist of physical characteristics, but the physical is associated with a mental image and capabilities.

We will not go into the issue that beauty is something subjective, but obviously beauty standards change in times and cultures. Keep in mind that your body is not just a piece of flesh but an entity associated with emotions, desires, capabilities, etc.

Now, look in the mirror and ask yourself the following questions:

Who do I want to be today?

That's up to you. Do you want to be someone who inspires and motivates to strive for dreams or someone who helps you become a better person every day?

You can choose someone you admire or even someone who has succeeded at something you are trying to achieve.

You can be the leader who will lead your team to success, the teacher who takes the time to teach you, the friend who is always there to listen, the writer who encourages you to know yourself better and develop your creativity.

Or you can choose to be yourself, discover who you really are and make the most of your talents to reach your goals and be happy.

How do I want to be seen today?

How you want to be seen today depends on your goals, your mood and the occasion you are preparing for. Here are some tips that can help you figure out how you want to be seen today:

- **Define your goals:** What is your goal for today? Do you want to project a professional and confident image at work? Or do you want to appear more relaxed and comfortable on a day off? Defining your goals can help you establish the image you want to project.

- **Assess your mood:** How are you feeling today? Are you happy and energized or do you feel tired and discouraged? Your mood can influence how you want others to see you.

- **Consider the occasion:** What event or activity are you preparing for? The occasion may influence the way you want to be seen. For example, you may want to project a more sophisticated and elegant image for a formal dinner, or a more casual and comfortable image for an outdoor outing.

- **Think about your personal style:** What is your personal style, do you feel more comfortable in casual clothes or do you prefer something more formal? Your personal style can influence the way you want to be seen.

- **Don't forget to be authentic:** Make sure the image you are projecting is authentic and reflects who you really are. Authenticity can help you feel more confident and comfortable in your skin, which in turn can influence how others perceive you.

What emotions do I feel when I wake up?

When we wake up, our emotions can vary depending on our circumstances. You may feel a sense of relief to discover that you are still alive, a sense of energy as you begin a new day, a sense of excitement for the challenges and opportunities the day will bring, or a sense of calm and relaxation as you take a breath and appreciate the moment.

You may also feel sad or depressed. This is completely normal and common. Many people go through these emotions. The key is not to let these emotions control your life.

Make sure you seek professional help if you need to talk to someone or if these emotions become too intense. There are several resources available to help you, such as therapists, support groups and community organizations.

In addition, connecting with others, having activities you enjoy and living a healthy lifestyle are good ways to cope with sadness.

How can you channel your emotions in a positive way?

- **Accept the negative thought and let it go:** Do not try to avoid or deny that thought. This means that you identify the thought, become familiar with it, and accept it as part of yourself. This does not mean that you agree with the thought, but that you do not try to suppress the thought or deny it. This can help you release the stress you may feel from trying to avoid the thought or deny it.

- **Ask yourself if this thought is realistic**: If it is not realistic, try to find evidence that contradicts the negative thought. For example: "I don't have enough skills to get the job I want." This thinking is not realistic. There are many ways to prepare and acquire the skills necessary to get the job you want. You can seek additional education, take online courses, or even ask someone to show you how to do something. You can also work on volunteer projects to gain experience and increase your skills. These activities can help prepare you to get the job you want.

- **Challenge negative thoughts with positive thoughts:** Try to replace negative thoughts with more realistic and positive thoughts. Negative thought: "I am a failure." Positive thought: "I've had difficulties before, but I know I can overcome them". Negative thought: "I'm not good at this". Positive thinking: "I am working hard to learn this, and I am getting closer and closer to the goal".

- **Recognize your strengths and accomplishments**: Try to remember the accomplishments you have achieved and how you have overcome challenges. My strengths are my abilities to work hard, my creativity, my competences to solve problems, and my dedication to work. Make a list of your own phrases like these:

I am proud of the accomplishments I have achieved, including successfully completing a graduate course, winning an award for my work, and being chosen for an important project.

I am also proud of how I have overcome challenges, including finding creative solutions to complex problems, adapting to new situations, and taking on new challenges.

- **Practice relaxation activities to calm the mind**: They are an effective way to reduce stress and anxiety and allow the mind to focus on positive thoughts.

What are my strengths?

Each person is unique and possesses a set of **hidden strengths** that make them stand out from others. These hidden strengths may be different for each person, but some of the most common include: creativity, critical thinking, communication skills, leadership, perseverance, frustration tolerance, honesty, ability to motivate others, teamwork skills, and problem-solving skills.

There are people who are good at listening, who are good at cooking, who are good at making decisions, who are good at organizing teams, who are good at saving money or getting deals. There are also people who are good with children, at marketing or sales, at design or programming, at writing, and at problem solving.

Putting all of your capabilities to work begins with recognizing and valuing them. **This may include making a list of your skills and strengths**, as well as examining the achievements and experiences you have gained.

Next, you can identify how you can use your skills and strengths to create new objectives and achieve goals. This includes looking for opportunities to develop new skills, learn new things, and find ways to put your already acquired skills into practice.

Finally, it is important that you commit to continuing your practice and staying motivated to keep improving and developing your skills.

What area of my life needs some attention?

Identifying which area of your life needs some attention can be a personal and subjective process, as it depends on your goals, needs and desires. However, below are some guidelines that can help you identify areas of your life that may need attention:

- **Make an overall assessment of your life:** and ask yourself in which areas you feel satisfied and in which areas you would like to see improvements. You can evaluate different areas, such as your physical and emotional health, relationships, career, finances and free time.

- **Listen to your emotions:** and pay attention to how you feel in different areas of your life. If you feel anxious, dissatisfied or discouraged in a certain area, it may be a sign that that area needs attention.

- **Identify your goals and objectives:** Identify your short- and long-term goals and objectives in different areas of your life. If you notice that you are not making progress on any of these goals, it may be a sign that that area needs attention.

- **Ask for feedback:** Ask people you trust, such as friends or family, for feedback on areas of your life that need attention. Sometimes it is difficult to identify our own weaknesses and areas for improvement, so getting feedback can be helpful.

- **Do an analysis of your daily routines:** and ask yourself if you are devoting enough time and energy to the different areas of your life. If you notice that you are devoting most of your time to one area, it may be a sign that other areas need attention.

How can I do something good for myself today?

You can do something good for yourself today by taking some time only for you. You can do something that makes you feel good, like reading a book, exercising, spending time with friends or family, taking a nap, or just relaxing. Or just do nothing. Doing nothing for short periods of time can be very rewarding. It allows us to detach for a moment from worries, problems and focus on the absolute present. And after a period of doing nothing, the mind and body are recharged with energy and we can feel our desire to do things double. So, **don't be afraid of idleness**.

The goal is to find positive activities that make you feel good about yourself. Sometimes we find out what we want and need to do, while telling ourselves we don't have enough time for it. Certainly we are all busy but there are some ways to optimize your time.

- Set priorities and try to do only what is really important.

- Set limits and explain them to others your priorities.
- Set a schedule and don't commit to more than you can accomplish.

- Take regular breaks so that your mind and body can recover and be ready to do the next jobs.

- Try to disconnect from technology for a few minutes a day.

- Make a schedule for yourself. You'll see that there are gaps that you can fill with activities for yourself. Or you can rearrange things so that some minutes are exclusively yours.

Time is your most precious commodity, use it wisely and put yourself as a priority. That way you will be able to dedicate quality time to your loved ones, your projects and hobbies.

STEP TWO:
ACCEPT YOUR MISTAKES

There are beautiful memories that we want to keep. But there are others that we don't. We shouldn't carry the burden of past memories that don't benefit us.

It is very difficult to forget something when we are thinking about forgetting it. On the other hand, we forget things when they do not weigh on us and only later they reappear because someone brings them to our memory.

Memory is tricky and we cannot control it, but we can train ourselves to know that there are things we can let go of our mind, without forcing them: a painful event, a mistake, a failure, disappointments and betrayals.

We do not always have to remember what torments us. In order to be able to forget something, it is important that you give yourself the time to process what happened and allow yourself to feel all the emotions that arise.

Accept the past because it can no longer be changed. Certainly, it is difficult to accept that something that happened can no longer be changed, but doing that is vital in order to move forward. Sometimes, the best thing you can do is to let go of what is causing you pain and accept that there are things you cannot control.

Part of your past is your mistakes or those things you regret. But you can't change any of that. You can change your attitude so as not to repeat mistakes, but what was done you have to try to leave it behind. Do not torment yourself for the mistakes of the past. Examine them frankly but let them go. **Be fair but not cruel**.

You are more than your mistakes, setbacks and stumbles.

You are a passionate person, with unique talents and skills, with goals and dreams you want to achieve.

You are made of moments and memories, smiles and tears, experiences and learning.

You make mistakes because all human beings make mistakes, and very often.

It doesn't matter if you have failed in the past; what matters is that you have the courage to move forward.

Mistakes are wounds, but they are also valuable lessons for the future. You have the power to forgive yourself and transform mistakes into successes. You are strong enough to endure whatever life throws at you and persevere to realize your dreams.

Failures are necessary to learn from mistakes and improve. Failures give us the opportunity to learn and grow as people, and help us gain a different perspective on our goals and our life. By failing, we realize that there are other ways to achieve our goals, and that the only way to achieve success is through effort and persistence.

Failures allow us to acquire new skills and discover new ways of thinking, which helps us to improve our skills and become better people. They also help us develop resilience and patience, which are necessary to achieve success.

Try these four simple things:

- Learn how to learn from mistakes instead of beating you up about them.

- Give yourself credit for your accomplishments and don't compare yourself to others.

- Set achievable goals and limit yourself to small steps.

- Surround yourself with positive, supportive people who will help you find the best path for you.

Sometimes we are not able to forgive ourselves and we carry our guilt. In general, our mistakes and sins (to call them somehow) are bearable. A dictator, a serial killer or a genocide are not the readers of this book, that is another thing.

But your mistakes are probably very common and even if they have annoyed others or hurt them they may not be unforgivable. That, of course, only you know. We are referring to the mistakes and faults we make as a couple, family, workers, citizens. It does not mean that there are no consequences and that there are people hurt by our faults, our indifference or negligence. But **what is done is done. It is a truth that we cannot change**. And sometimes you may feel that you messed up your life and that you don't deserve forgiveness from anyone, not even from yourself. It's normal to feel that way.

Forgiving yourself is a difficult process and sometimes can take time. The most important thing is that you strive to be self-compassionate and give yourself permission to feel freely what you feel, without repressing or masking it.

There will undoubtedly be a lot of things that you have to put aside. This includes people, situations, attitudes and behaviors. Learn to identify what is unhealthy for you and make the decision to let it go.

The art of accepting yourself is also the ability to erase things, as if we were editing our own life.

A final note on self-forgiveness

Buddhists practice self-compassion. This practice is based on the principle that we are all imperfect human beings and that each of us deserves love and compassion. Self-compassion involves being kind and compassionate to oneself, accepting and embracing negative feelings, and treating oneself with kindness and compassion.

It is about being aware of one's own feelings and treating oneself with the same love and compassion that one would offer to a friend.

Being self-compassionate means allowing yourself to have feelings, accepting your mistakes and trying to learn from them, and giving yourself the time and space to heal and grow. It also means giving you permission to take care of yourself and your needs. In general, it means allowing yourself to be human, with all your faults and virtues.

Being compassionate with yourself (and objective at the same time) may seem like a difficult task, but it is possible. The key is to **find a balance between self-care and personal responsibility**.

That involves being kind and loving to yourself, without judging or criticizing in a negative way. You can practice self-compassion through techniques such as meditation, mindful breathing and positive self-discipline. These practices can help you accept your emotions and thoughts without judgment.

Also implicates being honest and realistic about your abilities, strengths and weaknesses. You can be objective with yourself through self-reflection, self-evaluation and constructive feedback.

Balancing compassion and objectivity can help you address your challenges and difficulties effectively and maintain a balanced and realistic perspective on yourself and your circumstances. You can practice self-compassion and objectivity at the same time by reminding yourself that you are an imperfect but capable human being, and that you deserve kindness, respect, and personal responsibility.

STEP THREE:
ACCEPT YOUR ACHIEVEMENTS

Sharing your accomplishments with others, whether it's your friends, family or colleagues, is a great way to motivate you to keep going and to show your pride in what you've achieved. Remember that success is much sweeter when it is shared. By sharing your successes with others, you will be opening the door for others to better understand your talents, skills and motives. This can be a great boost to your enthusiasm and motivation to achieve even more.

Keep a record of your accomplishments so that you can read them over time later, on days when you feel you have not accomplished anything.

Write down a list of your most important achievements since you started your career, for example. You can divide them by categories, such as work, studies, skills, etc. Try to be as specific and detailed as you can, as this information will help you see the greatness of your accomplishments and describe them better. When you have finished your list, spend some time rereading it and reflecting on how far you have come since the beginning. This will help you **stay motivated when you're not at your best**.

As an additional practice, you can also write a list of all the things you want to accomplish. That list will help you design specific action plans for concrete goals.

Believe it or not, many of us find it harder to accept successes than mistakes. There is a culture that we should not make mistakes and that getting something right is the natural thing to do, so many do not recognize, much less celebrate their small day-to-day achievements.

Success gives us a lot of satisfaction. Recognize it and brag about it is a good way to better understand the fruits of our labor and development. Successes motivate us to keep striving in our projects and remind us that all the hard work we put in has its rewards.

Achievements can also be rewarded with something additional , as a kind of prize. The rewards you deserve don't have to come from others. Above all, they should come from you.

Rewarding yourself can include things like taking a day off to relax, buying something you like, going out with friends, seeing a movie, doing something fun, etc. These rewards will help you to motivate and feel good about what you have accomplished.

Some examples:

- A dinner at your favorite restaurant.

- One night's accommodation in a luxury hotel.

- A gift card to spend at your favorite stores.

- A luxury spa session.

- An annual subscription to a magazine or streaming service of your choice.

- An outing for two to a vacation destination.

- A ticket for a movie or play of your choice.

- A family picnic.

They are small but well-deserved rewards for your actions. If you gradually implement these incentives for what you achieve, your life will be more pleasant, and you will accept yourself in a fuller way and every day you will be happier with the person you are.

STEP FOUR:
ACCEPT THE EXISTENCE OF PAIN AND FEAR

Pain is an inevitable part of life. Although it can be difficult to cope with, is a natural part of the human experience and can serve as an opportunity to learn and grow. Recognizes that pain can be a motivating force to seek solutions and find happiness.

Accepting pain is a difficult process, but it is an important step in moving forward. First, it is important to **recognize that pain exists and that it cannot be avoided**. Next, try to understand the source of the pain and accept that not always it cannot be changed. Finally, try to find ways to cope with the pain, such as meditation, exercise, therapy, support from friends and family, etc.

Pain teaches us to be stronger, to be more resilient, to be more aware of our emotions and to learn to manage them in a healthy way. **Pain is an old master that teaches us to appreciate life and to value what we have**. It helps us learn to be stronger and not to give up in the face of difficulties. Grief teaches us to be more compassionate with others and to understand that we all go through difficult times. Also helps us grow as people and learn to face life's challenges.

We all experience pain in one form or another, whether it is physical, emotional or mental. Sometimes pain can be a difficult experience to deal with, but it is important to remember that pain is temporary and there are ways to learn to cope with it.

Pain is a form of the body's natural response to stress or physical or emotional discomfort. Pain is a basic emotion like sadness, fear or joy, and as such, is an inherent part of human nature. People react to different levels of pain in different ways. Some people may resist pain better than others, while some may tolerate it better over time. Pain is a subjective experience that is associated with feelings of distress, anxiety and hopelessness, and can also lead to a heightened sense of depression or intolerance. Although pain is natural, it is not something to be enjoyed, nor should it make us prisoners.

We do not all react in the same way to physical or emotional pain, as we are all different.

Pain thresholds refer to the individual's ability to perceive pain. These thresholds can vary widely among individuals, and can also vary based on age, gender, mental health and environmental factors. Some common factors that influence a pain threshold include stress, hormonal changes, anxiety and fatigue.

In the case of emotional pain, responses vary greatly from person to person. Some may react with anger or anxiety while others may opt for self-pity or denial. How each individual copes with emotional pain depends on many factors, such as the person's life story, beliefs, environment, mental health status, etc.

Some ways to cope with pain are:

- **Reconnect with yourself:** To heal spiritual pain, you must first reconnect with yourself. Acknowledging your feelings will help you understand them better and make better decisions. Practice a guided meditation to connect with the deep part of your inner self.

- **Connect with nature:** Spend time in nature to heal your spirit and to relieve your body. Breathe in the fresh air, listen to the sounds of nature, smell the fragrance of flowers and observe the beauty of nature. This can help you feel calm and relaxation.

- **Develop your creative skills:** It include things like painting, singing, writing, playing an instrument, etc. These activities allow your spirit to express its true nature and connect with the world.

- **Share your feelings:** This is vital to healing your spirit. Find someone to confide in, someone who can listen to you and provide understanding. If you have no one, do it for yourself. Just talk to yourself and tell yourself what you need.

- **Practice gratitude:** Practicing gratitude is an excellent way to heal spiritual pain. Take time to remember the things you are grateful for, the good things you have experienced in the past. Learn to recognize and accept all your blessings.

Keep in mind that some types of pain will never go away (chronic physical pain, grieving for a child, a sibling, a parent), but over time you can learn that those painful feelings will still be there and that despite them your life can go on and you can even smile at other things and celebrate just being alive.

Humans feel fear as a natural response to a threat or potentially dangerous situation. This is a form of natural protection to help us prepare for fight or flight. Fear helps us detect possible shortcuts, warns us of potential dangers and prepares us for action. Our brain responds quickly to these signals and releases neurotransmitters, which allow us to react effectively to the stimuli around us. This fear response helps ensure our survival by providing mental and physical alertness so that we can react quickly when a real threat presents itself.

Some people experience excessive levels of fear, which can be extremely paralyzing. Excessive fear can be rooted in past trauma, anxiety or stress, and can manifest in phobias, anxiety disorders or panic. Sometimes, attempts to cope with and overcome the fear can make the situation feel even more overwhelming.

Fear can be learned through experience, observation, environment or teaching. Humans learn fear by experiencing feared situations or by observing how others react to fear.

The **environment can also influence fear learning**. From childhood, certain fears are learned, such as the fear of lacking money, love or affection. There are many ways people can learn fear, whether through scolding and punishment or by listening to anecdotes or stories about what to fear. And even if they are inherited and false fears, we carry them with us as absolute truths.

Illusory fears are those based on unfounded fears or outdated sensations caused by imagination or prejudice. Many times, these fears feel authentic or real to those who experience them and have a range of emotional impacts. These fears are generally not based on real events but rather on fearful ideas or fantasies. Some common examples are fears of flying, public speaking, heights, social insecurities, such as imposter 'syndromes' and many more. These fears, although not biologically real, can have real consequences for those who suffer from them and need treatment to deal with them.

You must work to deal with your fears before they become phobias. In order to do that you should immerse yourself in them rather than avoid them. For example, if you are afraid of insects, look up comprehensive information about them and try to see one up close. If you are afraid to express what you think to others, try ways of saying it little by little. If you are afraid of speaking in public, start with a small audience of just one person and then increase the number of listeners. If you are afraid of any political faction, read more about their positions and thoughts and talk to a representative who can make you understand that they are not a threat to you. It is important for you to know that facing your fears, but that does not mean you should expose yourself to anything dangerous.

Knowledge is the best weapon against irrational fears.

It is natural to be afraid of things we cannot understand even though we can accept them. For example, the fear of death that from time to time haunts many of us. Regardless of our religious or philosophical beliefs we have all had one or many times fear of the inevitable end of our lives.

Some say that you should live life as if it were your last day. In reality, in one day you will do little except get depressed if it really is your last. **Don't live life as the last day, live life as the last year and live each day as if it were the first one**.

Live life intensely, enjoy every moment to the fullest, cultivate yourself as a person, explore new experiences that will help you grow, encourage yourself to try things that will keep you adventurous and fulfilled, surround yourself with good and supportive people, laugh a lot and pursue your dreams. To live intensely is to live without limitations or fears, is to take risks and be happy.

Death is an inevitable part of life, so it is important to **live with love of life and not with fear of death**. Living in fear of death can prevent you from making the most of your life, while living with love of life gives you the freedom to enjoy your life to the fullest.

By accepting death as a natural part of life, you can also make the most of the time you have here.

It is not about living in fear of death but in love of life.

Death is not something to fear, but something to accept. Death is a natural part of life, and there is nothing we can do to avoid it. Therefore, instead of fearing it, we should accept it and live our lives with love and gratitude. This will allow us to live with purpose.

Take advantage of each day to do something meaningful, such as spending time with loved ones, doing something you enjoy, learning something new, etc. Life is short, so don't waste time by doing what you don't like or living to please others.

How to get the most out of life? Here are some ideas:

- **Learn something new every day:** It can be a new skill, a new word or a new subject. Never stop expanding your knowledge.

- **Set goals:** Set short, medium and long term goals. This will help you stay motivated and allow you to see what you have achieved.

- **Surround yourself with positive people:** Positive people will help you see life in a different way and motivate you to achieve your goals.

- **Live in the present:** Seize the present moment and enjoy the good things life has to offer. Understand that every moment passes with no turning back.

- **Do what you love:** Find something you love to do and dedicate yourself to it. This will help you make the most of your time.

- **Take care of your health:** Take care of your mental and physical health so you can enjoy life to the fullest. A healthy life is a fuller life.

- **Learn to say NO:** Don't overload yourself with work, commitments, tasks and things you don't like and don't have a duty to do. Be responsible with your work, your friends and your family, but set limits because there are things you have the right not to do.

- **Develop a positive attitude:** Develop a positive attitude towards life so you can enjoy it to the fullest. If you learn to look at the world with a smile on your face, the world is likely to smile back at you.

- **Learn to forget:** Not all experiences mark your life, nor do all failures, heartbreaks and disappointments define us or are forever.

Of course, there is much more. You know better than anyone what you want, what you like, what fulfills you in life. So just do it.

STEP FIVE: ACCEPT YOUR DARK SIDE

We all have our own inner demons, our own struggles and our own fears. Accepting that we all have a dark side helps us to better understand others and ourselves. If we can accept our dark side, we can work to control it and use it to our advantage.

It is important to **recognize that our inner demons can be a motivating force for us**. It is about fighting against that part of our nature that we don't like but is there.

To a greater or lesser extent many of us have doses of selfishness, greed, indolence, conflict, jealousy, malice. It is like that, we all have something that we do not like and that we know is not right. That is why it is important to be sincere and to be aware of these flaws. Accepting them is a way to combat and minimize them.

Our inner demons do not have to control us. We are the ones who must control them. **We are the mastermind of our body, our intellect and our soul**.

Especially when we don't know them, sometimes those inner demons can take over and make us feel sad, anxious or overwhelmed.

They can even make us hate ourselves. Such demons are the negative thoughts and feelings of inferiority that prevent us from achieving our goals and being happy, as they make us feel that we are not good enough and do not deserve success. Inner demons make us feel that we are not worthy of love and acceptance, preventing us from being ourselves and living a full and happy life.

Our demons can hurt others, both physically and emotionally, this can include manipulation, verbal abuse, constant criticism, chronic discontent and even physical violence. Such behaviors can have a huge impact on someone's life, both in the short and long term, profoundly affecting their self-esteem, their ability to form healthy relationships and their overall mental health. In the long run, hurting others is hurting ourselves, because the repetition of this behavior indicates to our unconscious that we are despicable.

Knowing these demons means that we control them instead of them controlling us, means understanding the hidden forces that affect us. This allows us to take control of our lives and make choices that lead to a more fulfilling life and to better understand others and ourselves, as we understand human nature and develop greater compassion and understanding for others.

We cannot always overcome these demons, but by knowing them we keep them at bay, that means being aware of our actions and thoughts and trying to avoid those that are negative or harmful.

You should try to avoid impulsive behavior, offensive language, violence, substance abuse, manipulative behavior, abusive behavior, acting out, and behavior that is harmful.

Look at yourself as if you were someone else. We are often told to learn to put ourselves in the shoes of others, but **it is also helpful to see others in our shoes**. That way of taking distance from ourselves makes us see ourselves in a more focused way, learn the good things we have, but also see what our dark side looks like.

We are more than one, **we are not the same person forever and we don't have to be**, including that child or young person you were and no longer were because you changed and left it behind. There is nothing wrong with being a new person every day or to try to be a new person in some areas.

The important thing is that you accept what you were, so that you can welcome a new you.

STEP SIX: ACCEPT THAT YOU ARE LUCKY

I am grateful for everything that happens to me, because I know that everything happens for a reason and it helps me grow as a person.

I am always grateful for the good things that happen to me. I feel blessed for all the opportunities I have been given and for all the people who have helped me achieve my goals.

I thank God for all the blessings he has given me and for the life he has given me.

Not all the good things that happen to us are because of our effort and work. Sometimes chance, fortune, divinity (or whatever you want to call it) is there for us.

We must recognize the place the fortune has in our lives. **Many good things happen to us because in some moments we simply have good luck**. That's all. And even if there has been no effort on our part we have to value and appreciate them.

Your birth itself, your state of health or your financial situation can be in good shape thanks to good fortune, that golden angel who cares about us. Of course, there is also that black angel that causes us misfortunes in spite of our will to avoid them, but we will not talk about that.

Keep in mind that **many wonderful things have probably happened and will happen to you because of chance**. It is like a lottery that we can win without having bought the ticket. The point is not to desperately seek to win that lottery, but to realize when we receive the prize.

Your sense of sight, your sense of hearing, your ability to walk or move, your opportunities to have studied or gotten a job are in part caused by that good fortune. Accept it and recognize it as part of your life.

Luck is an important factor in life because, although we cannot control everything that happens to us, some situations depend largely on luck or chance. For example, two people with similar skills and efforts may have very different results in life, simply because they have had different opportunities or found themselves in favorable or unfavorable situations.

Being grateful for our good fortune is important because it allows us to recognize and appreciate the positive opportunities and experiences that come our way in life. **When we are grateful, we can enjoy the good things that happen to us and foster a more positive attitude toward life in general**.

Gratitude helps us maintain a balanced perspective and appreciate what we have, rather than focusing on what we lack. When we are grateful, we can feel more satisfied and happy with our lives, and we can be more resilient to challenges and difficulties that may arise.

Being grateful for our good fortune can also foster a kindlier attitude toward others. By recognizing and appreciating our own blessings, we can develop greater understanding and empathy for those around us.

Gratitude can help us strengthen our personal and professional relationships. When we express gratitude to people who have helped or supported us, we can strengthen our bonds and improve the quality of our relationships. When you get up, or go to bed, or before you start your meal, give thanks. Think mentally about the things fortune has blessed you with and if you have time write them down on a piece of paper.

You can be thankful for thousands of things, here are some examples:

Opening my eyes this morning.

Having a bed and a roof where to sleep.

Good thing there wasn't a nuclear disaster.

The taste of the morning cup of coffee.

The text or voice message from someone I care about.

The TV series that kept me late at night… but happy.

The phrase I read in that book that was recommended to me.

The cash payment I just received.

The joke I was just told that made me laugh a lot.

The opportunities to help and contribute.

Breathing, something as simple and wonderful as that.

My cat, my dog, my plants.

Life as simple as that, in its pure state.

The list will be as personal and as long as you want it to be. You can even share some of the things you are grateful for with your loved ones to spread that energy of gratitude.

Believe it or not, you are much luckier than you think. Reflect on that. And accept as blessings of fortune everything good that happens to you, no matter how small.

STEP SEVEN:
ACCEPT YOUR ENVIRONMENT

Who we really are? Perhaps a generic answer would be that we are a unique group of people, with our own stories, experiences and perspectives; we are a mix of cultures, ages, genders, ethnicities, sexual orientations and beliefs. Collectively, we are a diverse, interconnected and collaborative community.

Have you ever wondered who you are besides your name? Many people answer it differently:

I am a unique person, with my own opinions and perspectives, and I strive to be better every day.

I am someone who cares and loves the people around me, and who seeks to be a positive contribution to society.

I am someone who shares my accomplishments and failures with others, and who tries to learn from mistakes in order to improve.

I am someone who believes strongly in goodness and justice, and who is always willing to help others.

I am someone who, despite challenges, always tries to move forward towards a better future.

You can craft your own answer, but beyond that it's about knowing what's underneath all those phrases.

Are you what you have decided or are you the result of your context?

The answer to this question depends on the perspective with which one approaches the subject. Some would say that we are the result of our context, as our decisions are influenced by the experiences, relationships and environments around us. Some could argue that we are the result of our decisions, as we are solely responsible for our actions. Both perspectives may have some truth to them, as our decisions are influenced by our context and, at the same time, we are responsible for our decisions.

There are things that only we like and that others reject, such as musical tastes, political points of view, interests. This is totally normal. Our tastes and ideas do not have to coincide with those of another person. After all, we are unique individuals and that means we tend to have particular preferences and opinions.

In reality, our tastes are shared, but there are also certain aspects that distinguish us.

For example, one of us may like classical music and the other electronic music. One of us may like outdoor sports, while the other prefers to stay indoors watching movies. One of us may like home-cooked meals, while the other prefers going out to restaurants. Some of us are conservative, some of us are liberal. Some of us are sensitive to ecological issues, others to economic issues. But despite our differences, we also share many things, such as a love of art, theater, travel, social thoughtfulness and political views.

In general, we like to lean towards some causes and reach out to like-minded people. And we feel somewhat uncomfortable when we interact with people who think very differently from us, especially on sensitive issues.

And sometimes this discomfort or inability to dialogue and tolerance creates a conflict that isolates us or, at the other extreme, can cause us to doubt what we think, what we believe or what we feel. It is worthy to listen to others, take into account their opinions and seek an agreement in which everyone agrees, but we should not feel obliged to accept what others propose. We should always stand by our convictions and make our own decisions.

Some people only relate to like-minded people to avoid conflict. They only are interested in having the same perspectives of life. Other more self-confident people seek different opinions, understanding and tolerance of differences, they have a greater ability to discuss and reach mutually beneficial agreements.

As always, balance is the key and we must try not to lose sight of our own desires and preferences, although it is important to take into account the desires and tastes of the other.

Maintaining our individuality when relating to others is essential to our emotional well-being and personal growth. To achieve this, it is important that we learn to set healthy boundaries and respect our own needs and desires.

First, it is important that we have clarity about who we are and what we value. **By having a good understanding of our own identity, we can establish healthy boundaries in our relationships and maintain our individuality**. At the same time, it is important to learn to listen to others with attention and respect, and to value your own perspectives and needs.

In addition, it is essential to establish healthy boundaries in our relationships, which involves saying "no" when necessary. This allows us to maintain control of our lives and avoid feeling overwhelmed or stressed by the demands of others. We should maintain our own interests and hobbies. By devoting time to our own activities and political interest, we help us maintain our individuality and nurture our own passions and goals.

Finally, it is important to learn to value and respect the differences between ourselves and others, and not to judge or compare ourselves to them. By learning to accept and value our own uniqueness, we can develop more authentic and meaningful relationships with others.

Different opinions do not have to be a reason to separate us. On the contrary, they can become an opportunity for personal growth and maturity. Diversity can be a tool for understanding, respect and comprehension in a relationship. If we are able to accept and respect different opinions, we can grow together and learn from our differences.

Sports, for example, can be a great way to bring people together , whether through participation in sporting activities, organizing a friendly competition or simply through a shared interest. Regardless of how the game is played, sport can provide everyone with many opportunities to have fun and connect with others.

Politics is a field of different interests and opinions. This can lead to heated debates and disputes. Many times, people oppose the opinions and actions of other participants and try to defend their own views. This dynamic can sometimes have the appearance of a fight, but in reality, it is part of the necessary process to reach a point of agreement.

The real way to manage differences of opinion is in the dialogue, based on the principles of justice, equality and freedom for all. This implies that dialogue is the means to build the consensus necessary to achieve the objectives of each of the groups involved. This may include negotiation as well as civilized debate, mutual understanding and respect for the diversity of opinions.

Dialogue, in the end, is essential for peace, development and prosperity. The ability to dialogue with people of different opinions helps us improve our decision-making skills and can help us find solutions that are satisfactory to all. In this way, we can build a stronger foundation for coexistence among people with different opinions, which is especially useful in modern politics.

It is easy to agree with those who have the same opinions, the real challenge is to dialogue, understand and accept those who think differently.

Some tips to have a fruitful dialogue are the following:

- Listen and understand the other person, try to put yourself in their shoes to better understand what they are saying.

- Use questions to go deeper into the topic and better understand the other person.

- Maintain respect at all times. Avoid excessive judgment or criticism.

- Clearly express your opinions and emotions.

- Return to previous topics of conversation to keep the discussion interesting.

- Be open to new ideas and opinions.

- Shows interest in the other person's issues.

- Share your experiences to show the other person that you can relate to him/her.

Many times, we deny ourselves the possibility of putting ourselves in other people's shoes, of seeing their opinions and letting their voice be heard and understood. This prevents us from having rich and enriching conversations in which both parties can express themselves and discuss ideas without misunderstandings.

Trying to walk in the shoes of others is a practice that opens us to an attitude of understanding and self-knowledge, as well as gives us a greater perspective on the lives and experiences of others. **It is a way to have empathy and to see reality from a different perspective**. We should get used to try to understand others, listen to their opinions, respect them and consider them in our decisions, and this will help us to develop better communication with those around us.

Sometimes is difficult to have the courage to admit that we may be wrong, **no one wants to think that their ideas are wrong or bad** and so we cling to them. Instead, it is more rewarding to examine our ideas from different angles to ensure that we are making informed decisions and weighing all the pros and cons.

But despite this examination, it is likely that we will continue to think very differently from the mainstream. This does not mean that we have to change (at least not in most cases), but that we must accept that the world thinks differently from us and that is a reality that we cannot change. Maybe our ideas and tastes are not the most popular, but that does not matter if we know that both worlds (the one around us and the one inside us) can and must coexist. That is what life is all about.

Accepting others means respecting and valuing people as they are, without judging or discriminating against them because of their differences. It involves understanding that **each person has his or her own story, experiences, values and beliefs**, all of which are valid and deserve to be respected. It also means recognizing that we all have strengths and weaknesses, and that we should treat others with empathy and compassion.

It does not imply that we always agree with them or that we have to share their opinions or behaviors. It simply means that, despite differences, we can find ways to coexist peacefully and respect each other. We must take into account the differences between people and accept them as something good to learn from. If we look for something in them that unites us as human beings, we will be able to establish meaningful relationships.

People are not only their tastes, their ideas or their opinions. **There is something else that makes us human and that is beyond language and customs**. This is where we meet and fraternize with our fellow men and women, no matter how different they may be.

Reaching this stage implies being stripped of everything we have learned and looking at ourselves with the eyes of the newcomer to the world, with curiosity, perhaps with some fear, but with the willingness to learn, to establish a bond.

Here are some guidelines that can help you to accept others:

- **Cultivate empathy:** Try to put yourself in other people's shoes and understand their perspectives, emotions, shortcomings, needs and experiences. This will help you to better understand their actions and decisions, and to develop a more compassionate and tolerant attitude.

- **Recognize and respect differences:** We are all unique and have our own experiences, perspectives, values and beliefs. Learn to recognize and respect others' differences without judging or discriminating against them.

- **Communicate effectively:** Listen to others carefully and to express your opinions and feelings respectfully and clearly. Effective communication can help avoid misunderstandings and resolve conflicts peacefully.

- **Cultivate an attitude of openness and curiosity:** Value differences and be open to learning from others. Curiosity and openness can help you expand your mind and develop more authentic and meaningful relationships.

Accepting ourselves through accepting others means recognizing that our differences do not make us less valuable as human beings, and that each of us deserves to be treated with respect and consideration. **By accepting others as they are, we are learning to accept ourselves**, including our strengths and weaknesses, our identity and our choices.

When we accept others, we are cultivating empathy and compassion, which allows us to see ourselves and others with a more loving and understanding gaze. At the same time, by understanding and respecting the differences of others, we are learning to accept our own differences and not judge ourselves for them.

STEP EIGHT: WRITE YOUR PERSONAL STORY

A personal story is a narrative of a person's life, told from his or her perspective and based on his or her experiences, emotions, thoughts and actions. A personal story may include details about a person's childhood, family, education, relationships, work, health, interests, fears, failures and accomplishments.

Personal storytelling is a form of self-knowledge and self-reflection, as it allows people to explore and understand their own lives and their place in the world.

Through the narrative of their personal story, a person can discover their strengths and weaknesses, identify patterns and trends in their life, and explore their goals and values.

It is also a form of connecting and communicating with others. By sharing their personal story, a person can make connections with others who have experienced similar situations, and foster empathy and understanding.

In addition, personal story can be a way to preserve a person's memory for future generations. By documenting and sharing it, a person can leave a lasting legacy for loved ones and society at large.

Write your personal story. Many are born and die without a story, without being aware of it. Although the events are there (because things happen to all of us) there is no story if it is not told. And only you can tell it by making it conscious.

Tell yourself who you are, what you want, who you were, who you want to be, what you have done, what you have failed at, what is important and what is not.

Think of yourself as a character in a book with desires, awkwardness, fears, motivations, things to do, things you won't do. All this fits in your personal story. There are also those around you, those who love you, those who despise you, those who value you, those who criticize you, and all those who are indifferent to you and all those who secretly admire you.

Writing your personal story can be a challenging task, but it can also be an emotionally rewarding and revealing experience. Below, we provide you with some guidelines that can help you write your personal story:

- **Reflect on your life:** Take time to reflect on your life and think about the moments and experiences that have impacted you. Make a list of important events, people who have influenced your life and the challenges and triumphs you have faced.

- **Choose a focus:** Decide what focus you want to give your personal story. Do you want to tell a chronological story of your life, or focus on specific themes or moments?

- **Organize your ideas:** Organize your ideas and experiences into a logical and coherent structure. You can use an outline or concept map to visualize your ideas and organize them in a logical order.

- **Write a draft:** Write a draft of your personal story, following the approach and structure you have chosen. Don't worry about the quality of the writing at this point, just try to get your ideas down on paper.

- **Add details and emotions:** Add details and emotions to your personal story so readers can better understand your experience and connect with your story in a deeper way.

- **Celebrate your personal story:** Once you have finished writing and reviewing your personal story, celebrate it and share it with the people you care about. Writing your personal story is a way to acknowledge and value your experiences and emotions, and can be a powerful tool for your own self-knowledge and self-reflection.

Your personal story is written every day, but you must elaborate it with your words, maybe before going to sleep or after waking up. Every day is a chapter, or just a scene, but remember that something always happens to you, even if it is small it is significant if you give it value.

Don't think about the ending because it doesn't have one, that is, you won't know it... and it doesn't really matter. From that story, what matters to know is what you are, what you are being, what you are leaving behind. And whatever the path is, it is your story, you cannot change many things, but you can learn to look at them. **That's what acceptance is all about, learning to see your world with new eyes.**

WORKSHEETS

Answer to some of these questions. You can write on a piece of paper or in a notebook.

This exercise, repeated many times, will help you to value and accept yourself more each day.

Over time, some answers will change, others will be the same. That doesn't matter, the crucial thing is that each time you respond it will be a new way of valuing yourself.

- What do I feel when I look in the mirror?

- What do I think my loved ones think of me?

- What is the most important thing I want to do today?

- What activity do I have pending and have put off for a long time?

- How am I going to enjoy this day?

- What do I like most about my body?

- What do I like least about my body?

- Who did I help today?

- Who do I want to be today?

- How do I want others to perceive me?

- What is my most precious asset?

- What self-thought makes me uncomfortable?

- What is my greatest success?

- What self-failure makes me feel uncomfortable?

- What am I afraid of?

- What am I very good at?

- What do I want to learn this week?

- What are the names of the ten people who matter most?

- What things mattered a lot to me five years ago that I barely remember today?

- What am I grateful for today?

If you enjoyed this book, spread the word.
Maybe someone right now needs it more than you
do. Thanks.

For more information follow us here:

https://www.facebook.com/the.wellness.factory.org

About The Wellness Factory

We are a publishing house whose mission is to disseminate the teaching of well-being as a human right... without pressure, without fashions, without stereotypes.

More books for you:

The Body Factor

Printed in Great Britain
by Amazon